A companion to
*How to Have a
Big Wedding on a
Small Budget*

The Big Wedding on a Small Budget PLANNER & ORGANIZER

Diane Warner

WRITER'S DIGEST BOOKS

Acknowledgments

I want to thank all the students in my wedding seminars who contributed toward the content of this planner. I also want to thank my editor, Mark Garvey, for his help in its creation and organization.

02 01 00 99 98   7 6 5 4 3

Library of Congress Cataloging-in-Publication Data

Warner, Diane
    The big wedding on a small budget planner and organizer / by Diane Warner.—1st ed.
      p.   cm.
  ISBN 0-89879-530-3
    1. Weddings—United States—Planning. 2. Consumer education—United States. 3. Shopping—United States. I. Title
HQ745.W367   1992
395'.22—dc20
                                                   92-15831
                                                    CIP

Edited by Mark Garvey
Designed by Cathleen Norz and Sandy Conopeotis

To Linda, Bob
and Karen,
my cheerleaders

Table of Contents

Introduction

So, there's going to be a wedding! Congratulations! And if you're dreaming of a big wedding, but you only have a small budget, don't worry. You can have that big $20,000 wedding, with all the frills, for only a fraction of that cost. It can be done, you'll see!

By using the handy fill-in-the-blank worksheets and the "Things to Remember" checklists, you will be able to sculpt an elegant wedding for only a few thousand dollars, and your guests will never guess it cost you so little.

What a creative challenge! What a satisfying accomplishment! I'm glad to have a small part in helping you with your plans. You're in for one of the most wonderful times of your life.

With the help of this planner, you will not only create an elegant and memorable wedding but one within your financial means.

Happy planning and good luck!

Diane Warner

1
The Wedding Budget

Wouldn't it be nice to know ahead of time how much your wedding will cost? Most families begin the planning before they have decided how much they have to spend and whether it's possible to stay within those dollar limits. I have proven, in my book *How to Have a Big Wedding on a Small Budget* and from feedback from the seminars I teach on the same subject, that it *is* possible to determine your budget ahead of time. And not only that, it is possible to have a large, elegant wedding on any budget, even a very small one. Throughout this planner I will not only help you stay organized (another key to staying on budget) but I will present cost-cutting ideas in each category that will convince your guests that you spent *more*, not *less*, than the average amount on your wedding.

The expenses we are concerned with in this planner, by the way, are those to be borne by you, as some of the costs may be paid by others. This workbook is designed so that you may keep track of which expenses are being paid by whom; therefore, your personal expense will always show as the dollar "total" in each category.

This brings us to the natural question: "Who normally pays for what?" First, it should be understood that it is not uncommon in the nineties to share expenses. Also, certain ethnic groups expect the groom's family to pay all expenses. However, you need a place to start, so here are the norms:

Normal Expenses of the Bride and Her Family

- The bride's trousseau (her complete wedding wardrobe)

- Services of a Wedding Coordinator

- Invitations and announcements

- Bride's complete attire

- All flowers, except those paid for by the groom

- All photography and videography

- All music

- Transportation of the bridal party to and from the church and reception

- All reception expenses, including cake, favors and liquor

- Bride's gifts for her attendants

- Bride's gift for the groom

- Groom's wedding ring

- Rental of awnings, carpet, kneeling bench, etc.

- Rental of ceremony and reception sites, including all lighting and custodial expenses

- Accommodations for bridesmaids, if necessary

Normal Expenses of the Groom and His Family

- The bride's rings

- A gift for the bride

- Gifts for the best man and ushers

- Accommodations for his attendants, if necessary

- Flowers: Boutonnieres for his ushers and himself; the bride's bouquet; the bride's going-away corsage and corsages for all members of both families, unless the bride purchases these as part of her floral package

- Bachelor dinner, if one is given

- Groom's parents' transportation and lodging

- Rehearsal dinner

Normal Bridesmaids' Expenses

❧ Their own dresses and all accessories

❧ Transporation to and from the city where the wedding will take place

❧ A gift for the bride

❧ A wedding gift for the bride and groom

❧ A shower or luncheon for the bride

Normal Ushers' (and Groomsmen's) Expenses

❧ Rental of their wedding attire

❧ Transportation to and from the city where the wedding will take place

❧ A gift for the groom

❧ A wedding gift for the bride and groom

❧ The bachelors' party, if hosted by the ushers or groomsmen

Normal Guests' Expenses

❧ All out-of-town guests should pay for their own transportation and lodging. The bride's and groom's parents may help secure reservations, and may also offer to pay these expenses if they wish.

On the next page is your *Master Budget* with spaces to list total expenses for each category of your wedding. Your expenses go in the first column and others' expenses go in the second, with the grand totals shown on the bottom of the last page. Don't fill in the *Master Budget* yet. As we work through this planner, you will determine the exact amount to be spent in each category of your wedding by filling out the budget worksheets at the end of the chapters. You will then transfer the totals determined by those worksheets to this *Master Budget*, giving you a grand total for your entire wedding. You'll see how easily it works as we go along.

Master Budget

Category	Your Expense	Others' Expense
Ceremony	75.00	
Reception		
Bride's Attire		
Bridesmaids' Attire		
Groom's Attire		
Groomsmen's Attire		
Flower Girl's Attire		
Ring Bearer's or Junior Attendant's Attire		
Flowers	450.	
Other Food Expenses		
Music		
Decor		
Photography		
Videography		
Incidentals		
Other		

GRAND TOTALS $ _____ $ _____

2

The Calendar

It is ideal to have at least one year to plan a large wedding; however, six months can be plenty of time. If you only have three or four months, it can still be done, but you will feel a little more rushed and you will be cramming all the "As Soon as Possible" duties into one month's time. Also, you may have to take second or third choice of florist, caterer, minister, musicians and photographer, and your wedding dress may have to be sewn or bought off the rack.

We planned our daughter's wedding with only four month's notice and we were very fortunate that we only had to take second choice in one category—the caterer.

As you use the calendar that follows, you should know there are some preplanning considerations to keep in mind. For example, don't set the date of your wedding until you determine whether or not your favorite clergyman is available. Also, the date of your wedding may have to be determined based on the availability of your preferred ceremony and reception sites. And if you decide to provide your own food and beverage for the reception, you will need to reserve one of the much-sought-after sites that allows you full control, such as those provided by historical societies; city, county or state governments; parks departments; chambers of commerce; departments of tourism; schools; universities or private parties.

If you decide to use a hotel, private club or restaurant, you will probably be required to order the reception food and drink, including the cake, from their kitchen and at *their* prices. This is something to consider before you make any major decisions regarding your reception site.

The most popular sites are reserved months, and even years, in advance. Therefore, if you want to save money on the cost of the site itself, as well as the costs of the reception food and drink, you may need to set your wedding date according to the site's availability.

The Wedding Calendar that follows has three columns for each task. Fill in the "Date Done" as soon as each task is completed; the "First Follow-up" and "Final Follow-up" columns are to be used to

confirm that each task "stays completed." For example, as soon as you reserve the ceremony and reception sites, you will enter a date in the first column. Then, a month later you will need to confirm that your reservations are still intact; enter the date of this confirmation under "First Follow-up." The "Final Follow-up" column is to be used when you make the last confirmation about two weeks before the wedding.

Wedding Calendar
What to Do When

As Soon as Possible	Date Done	First Follow-up	Final Follow-up
Determine your total wedding budget $3,000	July 6		
Select the date and time of the wedding	July 6		
Reserve the ceremony site	June 20		
Reserve the reception site	June 20		
Choose the members of the wedding party	June		
Decide on your wedding's theme and color scheme			
Schedule your engagement portrait			
Bride's parents should meet the groom's parents	May		
Select your clergyman or rabbi, and schedule an appointment			
Start compiling the guest list	July 6		
Begin planning the reception			
Select the wedding gown	May		
Both mothers should select their dresses (Mother of the bride selects hers first)			
Select the attendants' dresses			
Arrange for the junior attendants' attire			

Four Months Before the Wedding	Date Done	First Follow-up	Final Follow-up
Finalize plans for the reception food and beverage and cake			
Finalize plans for the reception decorations			
Plan your favors			
Complete guest lists			
Order invitations, thank-you notes and napkins			
Order the wedding cake			
Select a photography plan			
Select a videography plan			
Select a floral plan			
Plan your ceremony decorations			
If you select an "amateur" food plan, begin preparing food, including sheet cakes if you choose the "Dummy Cake" plan			
Arrange for volunteer or paid helpers at the reception			
If you select an "amateur" floral plan, arrange for volunteers			
If you select an "amateur" photography or videography plan, arrange for volunteers			
If you select the "free recital" music plan, arrange for volunteers			
Arrange for volunteers to help with the decorations			
Arrange for a guest book attendant			

Four Months Before the Wedding	Date Done	First Follow-up	Final Follow-up
Arrange for a gift attendant *Brittany Graves*			
Arrange for a host/hostess for reception *Grandma Martha*			
Arrange for two helpers to cut the cake			
Arrange for volunteers to transport any rented clothing, decor, chairs, etc.			
Arrange for a volunteer or paid makeup artist			
Arrange for a volunteer or paid hairstylist *mandy*			
Arrange for a volunteer or paid manicurist			
Arrange for volunteer or paid nursery workers, if desired			
Arrange for volunteer or paid parking attendant			
Arrange for transportation of the wedding party, relatives and special guests			
Arrange for gratis or paid accommodations for out-of-town relatives and wedding party			
If you select any of the "Free Seamstress" plans, arrange for a volunteer seamstress *Mom mom Rina*			
If you decide to have a "Dummy Wedding Cake," arrange for an amateur cake decorator			
Arrange for a volunteer or paid wedding coordinator, if desired			
Arrange for other helpers, as needed: Helper No. 1 _____ Helper No. 2 _____ Helper No. 3 _____ Helper No. 4 _____			

Three Months Before the Wedding	Date Done	First Follow-up	Final Follow-up
Make appointment for a physical exam			
Plan ceremony details			
Reserve the rental of the men's wedding attire			
Begin addressing the invitations			
Obtain actual signed contracts to finalize all arrangements with florists, caterers, musicians, photographer, etc.			
Register gifts with department stores			
Make out seating charts for the rehearsal dinner and reception and make out place cards, if desired			
Decide on the dance order for the reception			
Decide on the order of the receiving line, if you decide to have one			
Make arrangements for all items you want to borrow, rent or purchase in order to create your ceremony and reception themes inexpensively			
Begin writing thank-you notes for engagement, shower or early wedding gifts			

Two Months Before the Wedding	Date Done	First Follow-up	Final Follow-up
Purchase or borrow any of the incidental items needed, such as the ring pillow, garters and guest book			
Have a meeting with all your volunteer helpers to outline duties and distribute checklists of individual responsibilities			

Two Months Before the Wedding	Date Done	First Follow-up	Final Follow-up
Arrange to have volunteers get together to make pew bows, favors, etc.			
Make up a list of "must" shots for your amateur or professional photographer			
Select the specific music to be performed during the ceremony and reception			
Select gifts for your attendants _Summer_			

One Month Before the Wedding	Date Done	First Follow-up	Final Follow-up
Apply for the marriage license			
Keep the medical appointment			
Send a wedding announcement to the local newspaper			
Plan the bridesmaids' luncheon			
Schedule a final fitting for the wedding gown			
Mail the invitations			
Check on the plans for the rehearsal dinner			
Get blood tests			
Verify guest list and call the caterer with final head count			
Have a personal meeting with every professional you have hired, including florist, caterer, photographer, musicians and wedding coordinator			

Three Weeks Before the Wedding	Date Done	First Follow-up	Final Follow-up
Arrange for all the men renting tuxedos to be measured at the rental shop			
Pack for the honeymoon			
Arrange for someone to be responsible for transporting wedding gifts from the reception site to your home			
Two Weeks Before the Wedding			Done
Prepare toasts for the rehearsal dinner and reception			
Make up your list of last-minute "To Do's"			
Give a Change-of-Address card to the post office			
Write thank-you notes daily			
Practice your wedding day hairstyle, with veil			
One Week Before the Wedding			Done
Make up and mail a time schedule for everyone involved in the wedding			
Confirm one last time with all volunteers regarding their duties			
Confirm one last time with all the professionals with whom you have contracted, including florist, caterers, photographer, etc.			
Attend the bridesmaids' luncheon and give your attendants their gifts			
Have final fittings for bride's and attendants' gowns			
Confirm rehearsal plans with your clergy			
Pack well-marked boxes of supplies for the rehearsal, reception, dressing room, etc.			
Continue writing thank-you notes daily			
Make up an "emergency kit" to take with you to the ceremony site, including needle and thread, scissors, travel iron, safety pins, comb, mirror, tape, thumbtacks, mouthwash, etc.			

The Day Before the Wedding	Done
Finish packing for the honeymoon	
Have a facial	
Have a manicure	
Have your hair styled	
If dressing at the ceremony site, assemble all clothing, makeup and hairstyling supplies to take with you tomorrow	
Fill supply boxes with all last-minute items for the rehearsal dinner, ceremony and reception	
Rehearse your vows	
Take a relaxing bubble bath	
Eat and sleep well	
On Your Wedding Day	**Done**
Eat a good breakfast; take it easy on the coffee!	
Style your hair and check your nails one last time	
Allow extra time for applying makeup	
Start getting dressed two hours before the ceremony	
Arrive at the ceremony site in time for any prewedding photos; allow a little extra time before the wedding in case of last-minute emergencies, such as traffic snarls, etc.	

3
The Ceremony

The ceremony is much easier to plan than the reception because it is less complicated and there are certain precedents for you to follow.

First of all, you need a site for the ceremony. It can be the same site as for your reception, which will not only save money but time as well in transporting the guests and wedding party from one site to another. You will probably find the most inexpensive site to be the church or synagogue of which you are already a member. There will be a set fee for members that usually includes the services of a custodian and wedding coordinator.

Other inexpensive sites may be rented through sources, such as those mentioned in chapter two: city, county or state governments, parks departments, historical societies, chambers of commerce, etc. You need to choose the setting for the ceremony based on your theme and the weather. You may decide to get married on a beach, beside a lake or, perhaps, on a yacht. Or you may find a beautiful garden, such as the Rose Garden in San Francisco's Golden Gate Park. There are even wineries that will lease out their grounds.

In any case, you will need to compare sites, not only according to price, but also according to their available services and equipment, as well as their religious restrictions. I have provided worksheets in this chapter to use when making comparisons.

Once you have selected your site, you will need to create an "Order of the Ceremony." This will include all music to be performed and by whom, any payment agreed upon, and any readings. You will need to decide on the order of the processional and recessional and, of course, the most precious planning of all — your vows and the wording for your ring exchange.

To help you with your vows, here are examples of traditional and nontraditional wording:

Here Is Sample Wording for the Traditional Vows:

❧ I, John, take you, Cindy, for my lawful wife, to have and to hold, from this day forward, for better, for worse, for richer, for poorer, in sickness and in health, until death do us part.

❧ I, Cindy, take you, John, for my lawful husband, to have and to hold, from this day forward, for better, for worse, for richer, for poorer, in sickness and in health, until death do us part.

Here Is a Variation of the Traditional Vows Wherein the Minister Asks Each to Answer, "I Will":

❧ *The Minister asks:*
John, wilt thou have this woman to thy wedded wife, to live together after God's ordinance in the holy estate of matrimony? Wilt thou love her, comfort her, honor, and keep her in sickness and in health; and, forsaking all others, keep thee only unto her, so long as you both shall live?
John answers:
I will.

❧ *The Minister again asks:*
Cindy, wilt thou have this man to thy wedded husband, to live together after God's ordinance in the holy estate of Matrimony? Wilt thou love him, comfort him, honor and keep him in sickness and in health; and, forsaking all others, keep thee only unto him, so long as you both shall live?
Cindy answers:
I will.

Here Are a Few Examples of Nontraditional Vows:

❧ I, Robert, take you, Linda, to be my wife and by doing so, I completely commit my life to you, with all its sorrows or joys, all its defeats and victories, all its experiences of life; I hereby commit myself to you; this commitment is made in love, to be kept in faith, lived in hope, and eternally made new.

❧ I, Linda, take you, Robert, to be my husband, and by doing so, I completely commit my life to you, with all its sorrows or joys, all its defeats and victories, all its experiences of life; I hereby commit myself to you; this commitment is made in love, to be kept in faith, lived in hope, and eternally made new.

Here Is Another Example:

❧ Anna, I take you to be my wife from this day forward, to join with you and share our lives together, to give and take, speak and listen, inspire and respond, and above all, to be true to you with my whole life and my whole being.

❧ Justin, I take you to be my husband; I promise to stand by you no matter what is to come, to love and respect you, to care for you, to comfort you and to share all sadness and joys that lie ahead. I promise to be loyal to you; I pledge myself to you with all my heart.

Here Is the Third Example of Nontraditional Wording:

❧ I, Bryan, pledge myself to you, Christine, completely as your husband. I want you to be my wife. I will stay by your side in sickness and in health, in bad times and good times, for all the days of my life.

❧ I, Christine, pledge myself to you, Bryan, completely as your wife. I want you to be my husband. I will stay by your side in sickness and in health, in bad times and good times, for all the days of my life.

Here Is the Fourth Example:

❧ Nancy, I hope our marriage will be like the endless light from the sun, radiating warmth into our lives, to accept all children from God with love. May every day of our lives be full of awareness of our existence for each other. My heart is open and my soul rejoices this day as we become one.

❧ Richard, when I entered your life, I experienced love and happiness and now I want to be your wife. As the sun sets, indicating the end of one day and the beginning of another, so this wedding indicates the end of our independent lives and the beginning of a new and joyous life together. I will be yours forever.

Here Is the Fifth, and Final, Example:

❧ I, Jim, want you, Janelle, to be my wife; on sunny days as well as rainy, may we survive through every storm and season until there is no more life. I want you to live with me, to share your thoughts, your desires and hopes. I want you to be my lover, my companion and the mother of my children, the heart of our home. I will stand by your side in sickness and in health, for all the days of my life. I love you, Janelle.

❧ I, Janelle, want you, Jim, to be my husband; I promise to be true to you in sunshine and rain, through good times and bad, in my waking and sleeping, all the days of my life. I want you to be my lover, my companion and the father of my children, the head of our home. I will stand by your side in sickness and health, for all the days of my life. I love you, Jim.

Here Are a Few Examples of Wording for the Ring Exchange:

❧ Take this ring as a remembrance of our marriage vows and our faithful love for each other.

❧ With this ring I wed you; with my body I worship you; and with all my worldly goods I endow you.

❧ Take this ring as a symbol of my eternal love and fidelity. Please wear it so that all may know that I love you.

❧ Laurie, I give you this ring and place it on your finger as a symbol of my love for you and in remembrance of the vows we have just given.

❧ This ring, without beginning or ending, is the symbol of my undying love for you. As it is made of purest metal, it is a token of my purest love.

You can take any of these examples, whether for your wedding vows or ring exchange, and work with them until you come up with your own special wording. Obviously, the nontraditional wording can become very personal and tender and you will want to say exactly what you feel in your heart. You can take bits and pieces from any of these examples, mix them with wording of your own, and create something so unique and special you will have all your guests in tears. Use the worksheet in this chapter to write your very own vows.

You will also want to decide on the order of your processional and recessional. Here are the traditional orders for Jewish and Christian ceremonies, but you can create your own order for your unique ceremony.

For a Jewish Ceremony, This Is the Order in Which the Wedding Party Proceeds Down the Aisle Into the Synagogue:

1. Rabbi and/or cantor

2. Ushers/groomsmen

3. Best man

4. Groom, escorted on his left by his father and on his right by his mother

5. Bridesmaids

6. Maid/matron of honor

7. Flower girl escorted by the ring bearer

8. The bride, escorted on her left by her father and on her right by her mother

The Recessional for a Jewish Ceremony Is in This Order:

1. The bride on the right arm of the groom

2. The mother of the bride on the right arm of the father of the bride

3. The mother of the groom on the right arm of the father of the groom

4. The maid or matron of honor on the right arm of the best man

5. The bridesmaids on the right arms of the ushers

6. The flower girl on the right arm of the ring bearer

7. The rabbi and/or the cantor

The Processional for a Traditional Christian Ceremony Is:

1. The clergyman, groom and best man all stand at the altar facing the processional

2. The ushers/groomsmen

3. The bridesmaids (or each usher may escort a bridesmaid)

4. The maid or matron of honor

5. The flower girl

6. The ring bearer

7. The bride, escorted on her left by her father

The Traditional Christian Recessional Is in This Order:

1. The bride on the right arm of her groom

2. The flower girl on the right arm of the ring bearer

3. The maid or matron of honor on the right arm of the best man

4. The bridesmaids on the right arms of the ushers

Now, you're ready for your worksheets.

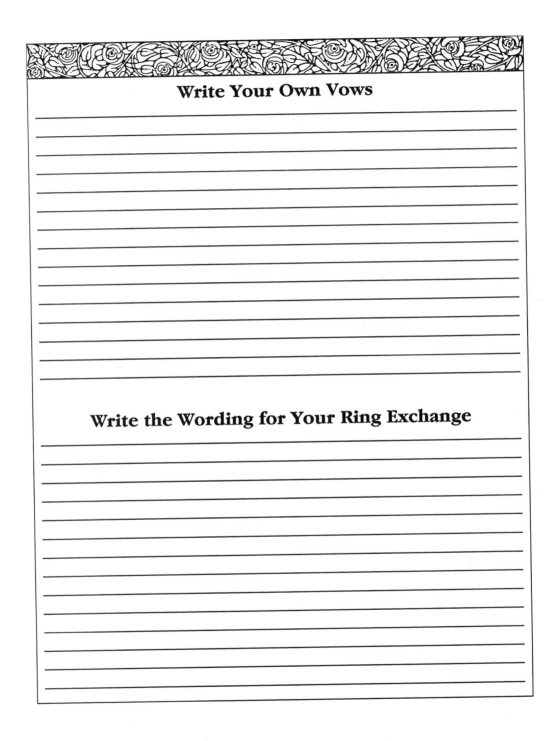

Write Your Own Vows

Write the Wording for Your Ring Exchange

Use this worksheet to record all readings, scripture, poetry and prayers to be used during the ceremony.

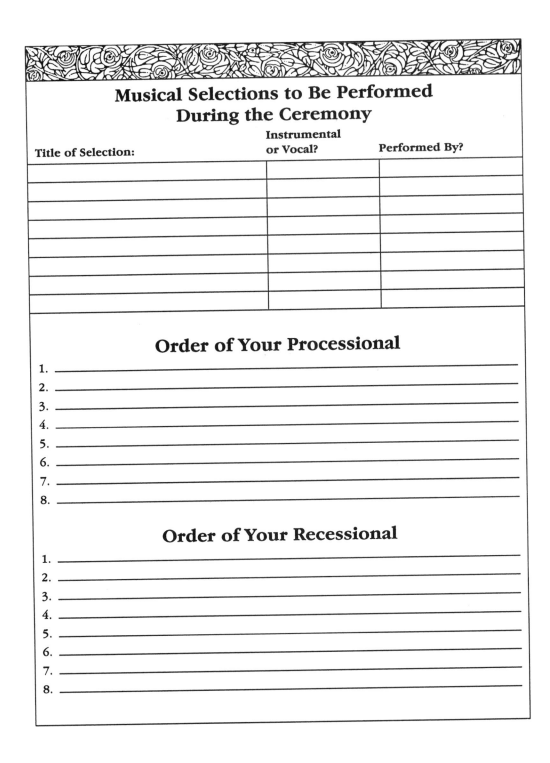

Musical Selections to Be Performed During the Ceremony

Title of Selection:	Instrumental or Vocal?	Performed By?

Order of Your Processional

1. _____
2. _____
3. _____
4. _____
5. _____
6. _____
7. _____
8. _____

Order of Your Recessional

1. _____
2. _____
3. _____
4. _____
5. _____
6. _____
7. _____
8. _____

Order of Your Ceremony

With the help of your officiant, write down the exact order of your ceremony, including all seating, candle lighting, processional, music, readings, prayers, poems, scripture, vows, ring exchange, recessional, etc.

Order	Participants
1.	
2.	
3.	
4.	
5.	
6.	
7.	
8.	
9.	
10.	
11.	
12.	
13.	
14.	
15.	
16.	
17.	
18.	
19.	
20.	
21.	
22.	
23.	
24.	

Rental of Ceremony Site

	Possibility No. 1 Name of Site:	Possibility No. 2 Name of Site:	Possibility No. 3 Name of Site:
Location of Site	Santa Rosa Bible Church		
Name of Contact Person			
Telephone Number			
Rental Fee			
Other Fees (Custodial, lighting, sound, wedding coordinator?)			
Equipment Available (Cushions, kneeling bench, etc.)			
Equipment You Will Need to Provide			
Services Available (Organist, altar boys, choir, etc.)			
Restrictions, if any (No smoking? No rice? No cameras? No aisle runner or elaborate decorations allowed?)			
Dressing Rooms Available?			
Existing Decor?			
Adequate Parking Available?			
Can Site Be Available Day Before the Wedding?			

	Possibility No. 1 Name of Site:	Possibility No. 2 Name of Site:	Possibility No. 3 Name of Site:
Dates Site Available			
Name of Officiant			
Advantages of This Site			
Disadvantages of This Site			
Other Notes and/or Special Considerations			

Ceremony Site Selected

Date and Time of Ceremony	June 17, 2000 — 1:30 pm
Location	Santa Rosa Bible Church
Fee	free
Deposit Required	no
Contact Person (Address and Telephone Number)	
Officiant (Address and Telephone Number)	
Services Provided	all
Equipment Provided	all
Counseling Appts.:	No. 1: Date: Time: No. 2: Date: Time: No. 3: Date: Time:
Location of Dressing Rooms	in foyer
Site Restrictions	none
Date Site Available for Decorating	day before
Existing Decor?	
Date Rental Agreement Signed	
Wedding Coordinator (Address and Telephone Number)	
Parking Provisions	

Special Considerations	

Use this page to staple any business cards, notes, copies of contracts, copy of ceremony program, drawings, etc.

Participants in the Ceremony

List every person involved in any way, including all members of the wedding party, all participants in the ceremony, ushers, candle lighters, officiants, musicians, etc.

Name of Participant	Address	Telephone No.

Final Ceremony Worksheet

	Who Pays?	Deposit	Balance Due	Total Expense
Site Rental				
Equipment Needed (Kneeling bench, etc.)	Reynolds			
Payment to Site Staff (Custodial, lighting, etc.)				
Wedding Coordinator				
Clergyman's/Officiant's Fee	Reynolds		$200	$200
Other				

Total Ceremony Expenses: $ _____

*(Transfer this total to **Master Budget** in chapter one)*

Things to Remember

❦ Selected your site?

❦ Deposit made?

❦ Balance paid?

❦ Met with site's wedding coordinator?

❦ Met with the officiant?

❦ Wrote your vows?

❦ Wrote the wording for your ring exchange?

❦ Selected your ceremony music and musicians?

❦ Selected your ceremony readings?

❦ Decided on the order of your processional and recessional?

❦ Wrote out the exact order of your ceremony?

❦ Designed a program for your guests, if you decide to have one?

❦ Rented or purchased any necessary equipment?

❦ Met with the site's lighting or sound technicians?

4

The Reception

The reception is more difficult to plan than the ceremony, mainly because your guests, who sat nice and still during the ceremony, arrive at the reception hungry, thirsty and needing to be entertained. This can all be easily accomplished, however, with careful planning.

Here are the things you need to plan:

❧ Rental of the reception site

❧ Rental or purchase of equipment, if necessary

❧ A theme and decorations

❧ Signing of the guest book

❧ Order of the receiving line

❧ The toasts

❧ Food menu

❧ Beverage menu

❧ Your wedding cake

❧ Musical entertainment, including the dance order

❧ Seating chart

❧ Special entertainment or presentations

❧ Favors

❧ The bouquet throw

❧ The garter throw

❧ The Getaway

❧ The order of the reception

The first thing on this list is the selection of your site. You can reserve a lovely reception site for less than $300 by using the ideas I discussed in chapters two and three. However, if you do find a reasonably priced facility, you may need to provide some of your own equipment, such as tables, chairs, an extra refrigerator, a generator, portable bathrooms, etc. Be sure to take this into consideration when you compare various sites using the worksheets in this chapter.

Your reception theme, decorations, music, flowers and favors are covered later in this planner, so your next task is to recruit a volunteer to man the guest book and decide on its location at your reception.

Next, you need to write out the order of your receiving line. Here is the traditional order to use as a guide:

Beginning with the first person to greet the guests.

1. Mother of the bride

2. Father of the groom

3. Mother of the groom

4. (Optional) Father of the bride

5. Bride

6. Groom

7. (Optional) Maid/matron of honor

8. (Optional) Bridesmaids

There will need to be a specific time set aside for toasts, usually started by the best man. If you decide to have a host for your reception, he may need to use a microphone to quiet your guests.

Now, we come to the food, beverages and cake—traditionally the biggest expenses of any wedding. Fortunately, these are also the expenses that can most easily be cut without sacrificing quality. The ideal is to keep your total cost to under $3 per person, and there are many ways to do this. My book, *How to Have a Big Wedding on a Small Budget*, has detailed plans, including recipes, but let me just give you an idea of what I mean here.

You will be very fortunate, of course, if you can find a caterer who offers a light menu that is affordable. Catering bids will vary tremendously, so be sure to call around.

If your family and friends are willing to help out, you can save a great deal on your reception food by using their contributions. Perhaps they will donate certain food dishes for your buffet table or you may purchase the food and have them prepare the dishes, saving the cost of a caterer.

Your local wholesale food supplier or delicatessen can be a big help, too. You can purchase the main dishes, such as trays of lasagne or meatballs and add the side dishes yourself. Breads, salads and vegetable trays are simple additions to your buffet table. By the way, always think in terms of "lots of bulk for little money." By this I mean, use pasta curls, macaroni or potatoes for salads. An inexpensive filler for sandwiches is to simply use ground-up baked turkey—it goes a long way for the money.

Don't forget that it is perfect etiquette to serve only cake and punch, especially if your reception will be held in midafternoon or after seven in the evening.

If you do decide to furnish an inexpensive buffet meal for your reception, the food can be presented professionally by creating a beautiful buffet table itself. Elevate the foods, fill the table with color (flowers, ribbons, candles and colorful fresh fruits), and garnish each food platter with lettuce; parsley; huge, fresh strawberries; or fresh flowers. You want your buffet table to be elegant, not "another church potluck."

In order to keep your table neat and filled with fresh food, you will need one paid or volunteer supervisor and three or four volunteer teenage helpers.

There are several ways to save money on the wedding cake. One popular idea is to use a "dummy cake" and donated sheet cakes. The cake on display at the reception is actually made from styrofoam layers which have been frosted and decorated with flowers, and because the cake is made from styrofoam, it can be as wide and tall as you like. I describe this cake in detail in *How to Have a Big Wedding on a Small Budget.* The guests are fed donated sheet cake from the kitchen, sliced onto little cake plates served on trays. Believe it or not, your guests will never even realize the "show cake" is never sliced.

Another way to save on your wedding cake is to purchase it from a private party or a supermarket bakery.

Whether you choose one of these cost-cutting ideas or order retail price from a bakery, use the worksheet in this chapter to record your decision.

If you decide to have dancing at your reception, you will want to establish a "dance order," beginning with your "first dance." Here is the traditional dance order usually followed at wedding receptions:

1. Bride and groom

2. Bride's parents

3. Groom's parents

4. Bride dances with her father

5. Groom dances with his mother-in-law

6. Groom's parents continue dancing together

7. Bride dances with her father-in-law

8. Groom dances with his mother

9. Bride's parents continue dancing together

10. Rest of bridal party joins the dance

11. Guests join the dance

Next, we come to the seating chart. You will need to decide who will sit at the Bride's Table and Parents' Table. This is the traditional seating arrangement. (See diagrams on following page for placement.)

Bride's Table

1. Ushers

2. Bridesmaids

3. Best Man

4. Bride

5. Groom

6. Maid/Matron of Honor

Parents' Table

1. Relatives or guests

2. Father of the groom

3. Mother of the bride

4. Clergyman

5. Clergyman's spouse

6. Father of the bride

7. Mother of the groom

Designate one or two tables as Grandparents' Tables; they may sit in any order they wish. The rule of thumb, however, is that all seating should alternate "boy-girl-boy-girl."

Any special presentations and entertainment, in addition to the bouquet and garter throws and distribution of favors, should be noted on the "Order of Reception" worksheet. This worksheet, by the way, will also help you establish a time line so the reception moves along at the right pace.

Use this worksheet to draw your seating chart

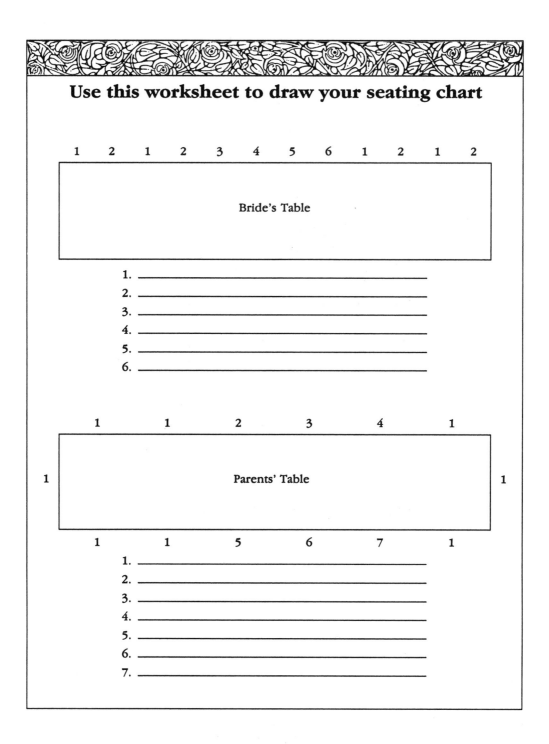

| 1 | 2 | 1 | 2 | 3 | 4 | 5 | 6 | 1 | 2 | 1 | 2 |

Bride's Table

1. _____
2. _____
3. _____
4. _____
5. _____
6. _____

| 1 | 1 | 2 | 3 | 4 | 1 |

1 **Parents' Table** 1

| 1 | 1 | 5 | 6 | 7 | 1 |

1. _____
2. _____
3. _____
4. _____
5. _____
6. _____
7. _____

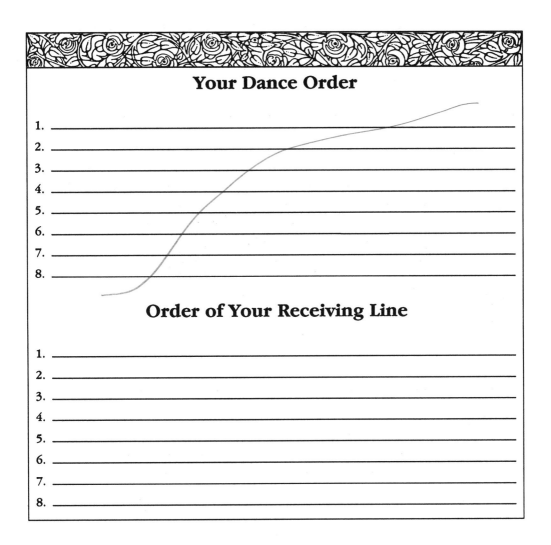

Your Dance Order

1. _____
2. _____
3. _____
4. _____
5. _____
6. _____
7. _____
8. _____

Order of Your Receiving Line

1. _____
2. _____
3. _____
4. _____
5. _____
6. _____
7. _____
8. _____

Order of Your Reception

Write down the exact order of your reception and how much time you will allow for each event, including the receiving line, buffet line, toasts, music, dancing, cake cutting, garter toss, bouquet toss, etc.

Order	Time Allowed	Participant(s)
1.		
2.		
3.		
4.		
5.		
6.		
7.		
8.		
9.		
10.		
11.		
12.		
13.		
14.		
15.		
16.		
17.		
18.		
19.		
20.		

Rental of Reception Site

	Possibility No. 1 Name of Site:	Possibility No. 2 Name of Site:	Possibility No. 3 Name of Site:
Location of Site			
Name of Contact Person			
Telephone Number			
Rental Fee			
Other Fees (Custodial, lighting, sound, wedding coordinator?)			
Equipment Available (Sound equipment, microphone, tables, chairs, etc.)			
Services Available (Valet parking, custodial help, etc.)			
Restrictions, if any (No smoking? No rice?)			
Adequate Parking Available?			
Dressing Rooms Available?			
Existing Decor?			
Will Site Be Available Day Before the Wedding?			
Dates Site Available?			

	Possibility No. 1 Name of Site:	Possibility No. 2 Name of Site:	Possibility No. 3 Name of Site:
Can Provide Independent Catering Service?			
Are Alcoholic Beverages Allowed?	no		
Any Music Restrictions?			
How Many Hours Is This Site Available?	until 6:00		
Maximum Number of Guests Allowed			
Advantages of This Site			
Disadvantages of This Site			
Other Notes and/or Special Considerations			

Reception Site Selected

Location	SRBC
Contact Person	
Telephone Number	
Date and Time of Reception	June 17 afternoon
Number of Hours Reserved	until 6:00pm
Fee	none
Deposit Required	none
Date Balance Due	none
Services Provided (Waiters, waitresses, bartenders, parking valets, catering, etc.)	
Equipment Provided (Microphones, tables, chairs, linens, table service, etc.)	
Equipment Rental/Purchase Required	
Location of Dressing Rooms	
Site Restrictions	
Date Site Available for Decorating	day before
Will There Be Any Existing Decor?	
Date Rental Agreement Signed	
Parking Provision	
Special Considerations	

Reception Food Plan Possibilities

Do-it-yourself plans or caterers' bids

	Possibility No. 1	Possibility No. 2	Possibility No. 3
Total Expense, including labor			
Name of Food Source (Private party, caterer, delicatessen, etc.)			
Name of Contact Person			
Telephone Number			
Equipment Available (Tables, chairs, utensils, linens, serving dishes and punch bowl, etc.)			
Services Available (Cake cutters, bartenders, waitresses, clean-up crew, supervisor, etc.)			
Advantages of This Plan			
Disadvantages of This Plan			

Reception Food Selected

Total Cost: $ _____

Main Dishes

1. _____   Source: _____ Cost: _____
2. _____   Source: _____ Cost: _____
3. _____   Source: _____ Cost: _____
4. _____   Source: _____ Cost: _____

Salads

1. _____   Source: _____ Cost: _____
2. _____   Source: _____ Cost: _____
3. _____   Source: _____ Cost: _____
4. _____   Source: _____ Cost: _____

Finger Foods

1. _____   Source: _____ Cost: _____
2. _____   Source: _____ Cost: _____
3. _____   Source: _____ Cost: _____
4. _____   Source: _____ Cost: _____

Other Side Dishes

1. _____   Source: _____ Cost: _____
2. _____   Source: _____ Cost: _____
3. _____   Source: _____ Cost: _____
4. _____   Source: _____ Cost: _____

Condiments

1. _____   Source: _____ Cost: _____
2. _____   Source: _____ Cost: _____
3. _____   Source: _____ Cost: _____
4. _____   Source: _____ Cost: _____

Cake

1. _____   Source: _____ Cost: _____

Beverages

1. _____   Source: _____ Cost: _____
2. _____   Source: _____ Cost: _____
3. _____   Source: _____ Cost: _____
4. _____   Source: _____ Cost: _____

Paper Products and Linens

1. _____   Source: _____ Cost: _____
2. _____   Source: _____ Cost: _____
3. _____   Source: _____ Cost: _____
4. _____   Source: _____ Cost: _____

Serving Bowls/Dishes

1. _____   Source: _____ Cost: _____
2. _____   Source: _____ Cost: _____
3. _____   Source: _____ Cost: _____
4. _____   Source: _____ Cost: _____

Utensils

1. _____   Source: _____ Cost: _____
2. _____   Source: _____ Cost: _____
3. _____   Source: _____ Cost: _____
4. _____   Source: _____ Cost: _____

Equipment

1. _____   Source: _____ Cost: _____
2. _____   Source: _____ Cost: _____
3. _____   Source: _____ Cost: _____
4. _____   Source: _____ Cost: _____

Other

1. _____   Source: _____ Cost: _____
2. _____   Source: _____ Cost: _____
3. _____   Source: _____ Cost: _____
4. _____   Source: _____ Cost: _____

Use this page to staple any business cards, notes, copies of contracts, etc.

Participants in the Reception

List every person involved in any way, including all paid or volunteer workers, host or hostess, musicians, catering company, bakery, etc.

Name of Participant	Duty	Address and Telephone No.	Paid Helper Or Volunteer? (If paid, how much?)

Final Reception Worksheet

	Who Pays?	Deposit	Balance Due	Total Expense
Site Rental				
Equipment Needed (Podium, tables, chairs, etc.)				
Food Plan				
Cake				
Beverages				
Cost of Personnel				
Other				

Total Reception Expenses: $ _____
(Transfer this total to Master Budget in chapter one)

Things to Remember

❦ Selected your site?

❦ Deposit made?

❦ Balance paid?

❦ Met with site's wedding coordinator?

❦ Rented or purchased any necessary equipment?

❦ Selected a food plan?

❦ Selected a beverage plan?

❦ Selected a cake plan?

❦ Selected a host or hostess, if any?

❦ Planned your seating chart?

❦ Planned your receiving line?

❦ Planned your dance order?

❦ Recruited all volunteers necessary?

❦ Signed contracts with all professionals involved?

❦ Prepared all foods possible ahead of time?

5
Attire

There is no purchase quite as much fun for the bride as her wedding gown! When other purchases are discussed, such as photography, flowers or reception food, the bride will usually smile politely and offer her suggestions, but when we talk about her dress, we have her undivided attention.

Every member of the wedding party, in fact, is understandably concerned about their attire, but the bride's gown is the most important purchase of all, for it will decide the formality of the wedding, as well as set the tone for the entire event.

Let's take a look at the customary wedding attire recommended for various degrees of formality:

Formal Daytime

Bride

White, ivory or pastel floor-length wedding dress with a cathedral or chapel-length train. Long veil should cover the train or form the train. Bride should wear long gloves if wearing a short-sleeved dress. Wear simple jewelry.

Bridesmaids

Floor-length dresses with simple caps or hats. A short veil is optional. Like the bride, they should wear long gloves if wearing short-sleeved dresses. The maid or matron of honor may wear a dress that matches the bridesmaids' or she may wear something that contrasts.

Mothers

Simple floor-length or three-quarter-length dresses. The two mothers' dresses should complement each other in style, color and length.

Men

Traditional: Cutaway coat with striped trousers, gray waistcoat, wing-collared white shirt and striped ascot.

Contemporary: Black or gray long or short jacket with striped trousers and wing-collared white shirt. A vest is optional.

Formal Evening (6 P.M. or Later)

Bride

Same as above except sleeves should be long and fabrics more elaborate.

Bridesmaids

Long evening dresses, fabric more elaborate than formal daytime wedding.

Mothers

Floor-length evening dresses; small head covering, dressy accessories (furs and jewelry).

Men

Traditional: Tails, matching trousers, waistcoat, wing-collared shirt, bow tie. (Ultra-formal: black tails and white tie.)

Contemporary: Contoured long or short jacket, matching trousers, wing-collared shirt, vest or cummerbund, bow tie.

Semiformal Daytime

Bride

White or pastel floor-length dress. The veil should be elbow-length or shorter.

Bridesmaids

Same as for a formal wedding, although cut and fabrics may be less elaborate.

Mothers

Same as for a formal wedding.

Men

Traditional: Gray or black stroller with striped trousers, gray vest, white soft-collared shirt and a gray or white striped tie.

Contemporary: Formal suit in choice of colors and styles, matching or contrasting trousers, white or colored shirt, bow tie, vest or cummerbund.

Semiformal Evening

Bride

Same as for daytime except the fabrics may be more elaborate.

Bridesmaids

Long evening dresses; fabrics may be more elaborate.

Mothers

Same as for formal wedding.

Men

Traditional: Black dinner jacket, matching trousers, black vest or cummerbund, white dress shirt, black bow tie. In warm weather, white or off-white jacket.

Contemporary: Formal suit (dark shades for fall and winter and light shades for spring and summer), matching or contrasting trousers. Bow tie to match vest or cummerbund.

Informal Daytime and Evening

Bride

White or pastel floor-length dress or a short dress or a suit. Short veil or bridal-type hat.

Bridesmaids

Same length dress as bride except that if the bride wears a floor-length dress, it is permissible for attendants to wear short dresses. Simple accessories.

Mothers

Street-length dress or suit.

Men

Dark business suit. In summer, white or natural-colored jacket, dark tropical worsted trousers, navy jacket and white flannel trousers, or a white suit.

Once you have set the time and theme of your wedding, you will have established its formality and you will be ready to go shopping. It is a good idea for the bride and only one other person to go shopping together. She may want to ask her mother or maid of honor for assistance, not only when shopping for her gown, but in the selection of all other attire as well. It becomes very nonproductive and frustrating to have all the bridesmaids along at once. If everyone hops together from place to place, trying on dresses and arguing over styles, you will not only have a wasted day, but a huge headache. To avoid this nightmarish possibility, make a plan ahead of time.

Have an idea of what you are looking for, not only when it comes to your own gown, but everyone else's attire as well.

Here are some cost-cutting ideas:

The Bride's Attire

❧ Wear a borrowed gown, if one is offered to you that you like and that can be altered to fit. This will only cost you the alteration and dry cleaning fees.

❧ Rent your gown. Many brides don't realize a quality gown can be rented for $75 to $225. Look in your Yellow Pages under "Bridal Attire," "Costumes," "Wedding Rentals" or "Rentals."

❧ Purchase a bridesmaid's gown in white or ivory. Many brides don't realize that bridesmaid's gowns come in these colors because they are almost never on display in bridal salons. Ask your sales clerk if a certain bridesmaid's gown can be ordered in white or ivory; if so, you will save several hundred dollars.

❧ Buy a "distress-sale dress" through the classified ads or a second-hand shop. Here is a typical classified ad: "Wedding gown, special order designer gown, size 10, never worn, originally $1,200, asking $200." I have seen beautiful wedding gowns for sale in resale shops for under $50.

❧ Have your dress sewn for you. If you have a volunteer seamstress in your family, the dress will only cost you about $120. If you hire a seamstress, it will add another $100 or so, still hundreds of dollars less than retail.

❧ Buy your dress discount. There are dozens of ways to do this: through a wholesale factory outlet, such as Gunne Sax, the J.C. Penney bridal catalog or you can use a discount service called "Discount Bridal Service." Call 800-874-8794 for the name of their representative in your area. This service can provide wedding attire, as well as accessories and wedding invitations, at 20 to 40 percent off retail prices.

❧ Bridal veils and headpieces can also be borrowed, rented, purchased at a "distress-sale," purchased discount or sewn by an amateur or professional seamstress.

❦ The bride's, as well as bridesmaids', shoes can be purchased discount through a catalog or at Payless Shoes.

The Bridesmaids' Attire

❦ One of the most practical ideas is to rent their dresses. This will cost each girl about $35.

❦ Have their dresses sewn for under $50 if you have a volunteer seamstress or about $90 if you hire one.

❦ The same discount ideas work for the bridesmaids as they do for the bride: J.C. Penney bridal catalog, wholesale factory outlets or the "Discount Bridal Service."

❦ One popular idea lately has been for the bridesmaids to purchase their dresses right "off the rack" from a women's wear store, such as Lerner's, Penney's or any local department store. The fact that the dresses are all alike will do the trick, even though they are not officially "bridesmaids' dresses." In one case recently, for the popular "black-and-white-wedding," each bridesmaid purchased a different, yet complementary, black-and-white dress. These dresses were suitable for everyday wear after the wedding and cost much less than an "official" bridal salon bridesmaid's gown.

Mothers of the Bride and Groom

❦ There is nothing wrong with borrowing a special dress for the occasion if one is available.

❦ The mothers' dresses can be rented, as well, at a cost of approximately $50.

❦ Their dresses can also be purchased discount from the same sources as the bride's and bridesmaids'.

❦ Their dress can be sewn for them, as well, which can save about $200 total cost.

❦ Another great source of dresses for the mothers is the "Finer Dress" section of the local department store. These dresses are usually much more reasonably priced than those in a salon, and, in my opinon, more flattering as well.

The Flower Girl

❦ Her dress can be sewn for $20 to $50, depending on whether you have a volunteer seamstress available or not.

❦ Her dress can also be purchased through a discount source.

❦ One of the best ideas is for the girl to wear her existing Easter or Communion dress, adding a big satin bow in the wedding color.

The Ring Bearer or Other Junior Attendants

❦ They can easily wear an existing Sunday school suit or white shirt, white shorts and a bow tie.

❦ The regular J.C. Penney catalog has complete sets of clothing for boys, including the suspenders, bow tie, jacket and pants for under $40, a purchase that can be used again after the wedding.

The Men's Attire

❦ The customary attire is, of course, a tuxedo. The only advice I have here is to avoid the designer tuxes, such as Pierre Cardin, Christian Dior or Henry Grethel, which all run higher in price to rent or purchase.

❦ The alternative to the tuxedo is for each man to wear a dark suit, even if he has to borrow one and have it temporarily altered. You will be surprised how uniform the men will look if they have matching bow ties, pocket hankies and boutonnieres.

❦ Whether the men wear tuxedos or their own dark suits, they can wear their own dark shoes. This will save the cost of renting them.

Following are worksheets for everyone except the mothers, who customarily arrange their own attire. There are worksheets for comparing the various cost-cutting plans, followed by actual cost sheets. The totals at the bottom of each of these final cost sheets should be transferred to the *Master Budget* in chapter one.

Bride's Attire

	Possibility No. 1	Possibility No. 2	Possibility No. 3
Location of Source			
Name of Contact Person			
Telephone Number			
Alteration or Seamstress Costs (if applicable)			
Rental Fee (if applicable)			
Purchase Price (if applicable)			
Costs of Fabric or Materials (if applicable)			

Bridesmaids' Attire

	Possibility No. 1	Possibility No. 2	Possibility No. 3
Location of Source			
Name of Contact Person			
Telephone Number			
Alteration or Seamstress Costs (if applicable)			
Rental Fee (if applicable)			
Purchase Price (if applicable)			
Costs of Fabric or Materials (if applicable)			

Flower Girl's Attire

	Possibility No. 1	Possibility No. 2	Possibility No. 3
Location of Source			
Name of Contact Person			
Telephone Number			
Alteration or Seamstress Costs (if applicable)			
Purchase Price (if applicable)			
Costs of Fabric or Materials (if applicable)			

Ring Bearer's or Junior Attendant's Attire

	Possibility No. 1	Possibility No. 2	Possibility No. 3
Location of Source			
Name of Contact Person			
Telephone Number			
Alteration or Seamstress Costs (if applicable)			
Purchase Price (if applicable)			
Costs of Fabric or Materials (if applicable)			

Men's Attire

	Possibility No. 1	Possibility No. 2	Possibility No. 3
Location of Source			
Name of Contact Person			
Telephone Number			
Alteration or Seamstress Costs (if applicable)			
Rental Fee (if applicable)			
Purchase Price (if applicable)			
Costs of Fabric or Materials (if applicable)			

Use this page to staple any business cards, notes, copies of contracts, brochures, fabric swatches, photos, etc.

Final Bride's Attire Worksheet

Item and Source	Who Pays?	Deposit	Balance Due	Total Expense
Gown				
Veil/Headpiece				
Shoes/Hose				
Petticoat/Slip				
Jewelry				
Other Accessories				
Alterations				

Total Bridal Attire Expenses: $ _____
*(Transfer this total to **Master Budget** in chapter one)*

Final Bridesmaids' Attire Worksheet

Item and Source	Who Pays?	Deposit	Balance Due	Total Expense
Gown				
Shoes/Hose				
Petticoat/Slip				
Jewelry				
Other Accessories				
Alterations				

Total Bridesmaids' Attire Expenses: $ _____
*(Transfer this total to **Master Budget** in chapter one)*

Final Groom's Attire Worksheet

Item and Source	Who Pays?	Deposit	Balance Due	Total Expense
Tuxedo or Suit				
Shoes				
Tie and Cummerbund				
Shirt				
Accessories				
Alterations				

Total Groom's Attire Expenses: $ _____
*(Transfer this total to **Master Budget** in chapter one)*

Final Groomsmen's Attire Worksheet

Item and Source	Who Pays?	Deposit	Balance Due	Total Expense
Tuxedo or Suit				
Shoes				
Tie and Cummerbund				
Shirt				
Accessories				
Alterations				

Total Groomsmen's Attire Expenses: $ _____
*(Transfer this total to **Master Budget** in chapter one)*

Final Flower Girl's Attire Worksheet

Item and Source	Who Pays?	Deposit	Balance Due	Total Expense
Dress or Embellishments for existing dress				
Shoes				
Hairpiece				
Accessories				
Alterations				

Total Flower Girl's Attire Expenses: $ _____
*(Transfer this total to **Master Budget** in chapter one)*

Final Ring Bearer's or Junior Attendant's Attire Worksheet

Item and Source	Who Pays?	Deposit	Balance Due	Total Expense
Dress/Suit				
Shoes				
Accessories				
Alterations				

Total Junior Attendant's Attire Expenses: $ _____
*(Transfer this total to **Master Budget** in chapter one)*

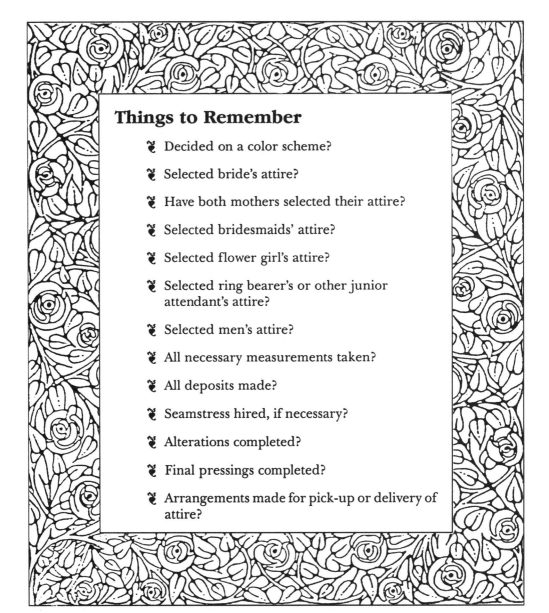

Things to Remember

- ❧ Decided on a color scheme?

- ❧ Selected bride's attire?

- ❧ Have both mothers selected their attire?

- ❧ Selected bridesmaids' attire?

- ❧ Selected flower girl's attire?

- ❧ Selected ring bearer's or other junior attendant's attire?

- ❧ Selected men's attire?

- ❧ All necessary measurements taken?

- ❧ All deposits made?

- ❧ Seamstress hired, if necessary?

- ❧ Alterations completed?

- ❧ Final pressings completed?

- ❧ Arrangements made for pick-up or delivery of attire?

6

The Flowers

Flowers have traditionally been an important part of the wedding ceremony. They denote celebration and congratulation; they fill the room with joy! A wedding without flowers would be like a day in traffic court—not very festive at all! You must have flowers, and as many as you can afford. You will find you can afford a lot more than you thought after considering my cost-cutting ideas.

Before we get to these ideas, let's take a look at a typical floral package available from a retail florist. A typical package deal will probably include:

- One bridal bouquet in colonial design, cascade design or an arm bouquet

- ~~Four~~ *five* total attendants' bouquets in these same styles

- Two mothers' corsages

- Four grandmothers' corsages

- Twelve boutonnieres

- Two altar arrangements

- ~~One~~ *four* flower girl basket

The price for this typical package ranges from about $500 in the lower-cost areas of the country to about $1,200 in the high-cost areas, but unfortunately these aren't all the flowers you'll need. The package doesn't include reception flowers or any extra corsages or boutonnieres for guest book attendants, favorite aunts or uncles, or the musicians, or floral arrangements for the pews, bannisters or altar railings. By the time you order everything you'd really like to have, you can easily spend $4,000.

By the way, if you do decide to go with a retail florist, be prepared to furnish him with the colors of the bridesmaids', mothers' and grandmothers' dresses; names, addresses and telephone numbers of everyone who will receive flowers; what kind of aisle decorations you want; and the delivery time and place for all the flowers he will provide.

Also, you will need to decide whether you want the florist to provide a kneeling cushion or bench, aisle carpet, candle holders, archways, trellises or other decorative items for the ceremony and reception.

There are several ways to save on your total floral costs and they are detailed in *How to Have a Big Wedding on a Small Budget*. One of the least expensive ways to cut costs is to use donated flowers and greenery. Perhaps your neighbors or friends have cuttings that can be donated to the cause. This, of course, means that you will need to coordinate the assembly of these flowers into corsages, bouquets and all the floral arrangements you will need in the sanctuary and reception hall. You can also save money by using silk flowers or by purchasing your fresh flowers through a wholesale flower mart. A bride can share the sanctuary flowers with another bride who will be married there the same day, or large floral arrangements can be rented very reasonably. You may want to use a combination of these cost-cutting suggestions.

Use the worksheets that follow to compare some of these ideas.

Comparison of Floral Plans

	Possibility No. 1	Possibility No. 2	Possibility No. 3
Name and Address of Source			
Name of Contact Person			
Telephone Number			
Costs			
Rental Costs			
Equipment You Will Need to Provide			
Services You Will Need to Provide			
Use of Existing Decor?			
Advantages of This Plan			
Disadvantages of This Plan			
Other Notes and/or Special Considerations			

Final Floral Plan Worksheet

	Who Pays?	Deposit	Balance Due	Total Expense
Retail Florist				
Do-It-Yourself Supplies				
Fresh Flowers (Wholesale)				
Silk Flowers				
Flowers for Cake Decorations/ Reception Decor				
Rental of Silk Arrangements/ Baskets				
Other (candle holders, etc.)				

Total Floral Expenses: $ _____

*(Transfer this total to **Master Budget** in chapter one)*

Use this page to staple any business cards, notes, copies of contracts, brochures, ribbons, floral bids, etc.

Floral Volunteers

List every person involved in any way, including your Free Florists; those who volunteer to help make corsages, bouquets, etc.; those who volunteer to help decorate the ceremony and reception sites; those who offer to loan you plants, trellises, etc.; someone to help distribute corsages, boutonnieres, etc. on the wedding day; those who volunteer to help with the transportation of rented arrangements, etc.

Name of Volunteer	Address & Telephone No.	Duty

Things to Remember

- ❦ Selected a floral plan?

- ❦ If you use a retail florist, have you furnished him color samples, names and addresses of all recipients, etc.?

- ❦ Recruited enough helpers?

- ❦ Purchased required floral supplies?

- ❦ Arranged transportation for all flowers?

- ❦ Arranged for someone to distribute corsages, boutonnieres, bouquets, etc. on the wedding day?

7

Other Food Service

In addition to the reception food, your wedding's biggest expense, you may have up to four more food-related considerations. They are:

- The rehearsal dinner

- Prewedding snacks

- Food for the houseguests

- The bridesmaids' luncheon (if hosted by the bride)

The Rehearsal Dinner

First of all, the rehearsal dinner is traditionally the expense of the groom's parents, who also serve as host and hostess for the event. Tradition has been thrown aside of late, however, and the rehearsal dinner can be provided by anyone—the bride's family, friends, other relatives, the bride and groom themselves—or it can be a potluck where the cost is shared.

If you want a formal rehearsal dinner that follows tradition, it will not only be a sit-down affair, but you will need to follow certain seating requirements. A traditional rehearsal dinner will also require centerpieces for the tables, place cards and proper toasts.

Just a word about toasts, whether at the rehearsal dinner or at the reception, this is the basic format for toasting: Everyone present, including the guests, is served a beverage. Champagne and wine are the traditional drinks, but it is fine to toast with a nonalcoholic drink as well. The drink is first poured for the bride, then the groom and then the maid of honor. The best man is always the last person to receive the drink.

The person being toasted does not drink along with everyone else but waits until everyone has had a sip. Usually men do the toasting, but it is fine for women to toast as well. Certainly the bride always returns her groom's toast to her, whether at the rehearsal

or reception.

First the bride is toasted, followed by a toast to the bride and groom. The first toasts are usually made by the best man, followed by the father of the groom.

If the rehearsal dinner is informal, which is very popular these days, toasts are still in order. An informal rehearsal dinner idea might be a barbecue, spaghetti dinner, old-fashioned picnic or even "Dutch treat" at a local restaurant.

If you do have a *formal* rehearsal dinner, here is the normal seating arrangement:

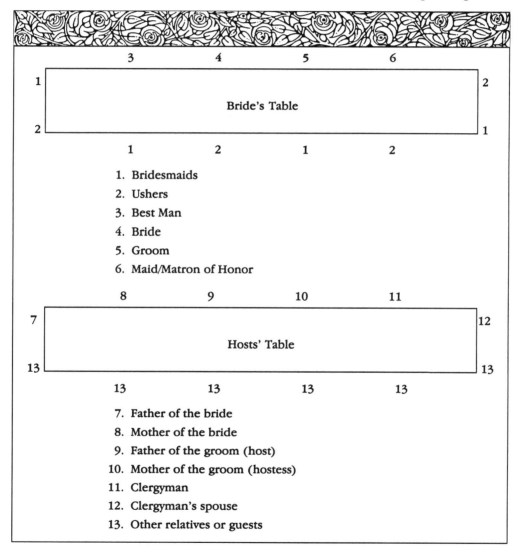

1. Bridesmaids
2. Ushers
3. Best Man
4. Bride
5. Groom
6. Maid/Matron of Honor

7. Father of the bride
8. Mother of the bride
9. Father of the groom (host)
10. Mother of the groom (hostess)
11. Clergyman
12. Clergyman's spouse
13. Other relatives or guests

Everyone who attends the wedding rehearsal should be invited to the rehearsal dinner, and it is very nice to send handwritten invitations; however, you may telephone your guests instead, if you prefer.

The host and hostess of the rehearsal dinner, usually the groom's parents, should be sure everyone is introduced to each other. The use of place cards can help everyone get acquainted, too; try to mix people up so the families and members of the wedding party meet each other.

You can turn the rehearsal dinner into a party by providing a little entertainment — perhaps a slide presentation showing the bride and groom as children, a comedy skit, or a light-hearted song with humorous words inserted that pertain to the couple or how they met. Use your imagination and you can make the evening very special.

Some cost-cutting ideas for the rehearsal dinner are:

❧ Families of the bride and groom "potluck" the dinner

❧ "Dutch treat" at a local restaurant

❧ Have a barbecue in your backyard or a picnic in the local park

❧ A "Do-It-Yourself Buffet," using prepared foods purchased from a wholesale food outlet or delicatessen.

Whether the dinner is formal, informal, catered, "potlucked" or "Dutch-treated," you can use the following worksheet to help with the planning.

Rehearsal Dinner Possibilities

	Possibility No. 1	Possibility No. 2	Possibility No. 3
Source of Food			
Name of Contact Person			
Telephone Number			
Menu Hors d'oeuvres —————— —————— —————— ——————			
Main Course —————— —————— —————— —————— ——————			
Salads —————— —————— —————— —————— ——————			
Breads —————— —————— —————— —————— ——————			
Condiments —————— —————— —————— ——————			

	Possibility No. 1	Possibility No. 2	Possibility No. 3
Desserts _____ _____ _____ _____ _____			
Beverages _____ _____ _____ _____ _____			
Decorations _____ _____ _____ _____			
Entertainment _____ _____ _____ _____ _____			
Total Costs Per Person			
Equipment You Will Need to Provide			
Services You Will Need to Provide			

	Possibility No. 1	Possibility No. 2	Possibility No. 3
Advantages of This Plan			
Disadvantages of This Plan			
Other Notes and/or Special Considerations			

Rehearsal Dinner Plan Selected

Address: _____
_____
_____

Contact Person: _____
Telephone Number: _____
Date/Time Reserved: _____

	Who Pays?	Deposit	Balance Due	Total Expense
Menu Hors d'oeuvres _____ _____ _____ _____				
Main Course _____ _____ _____ _____				
Salads _____ _____ _____ _____				
Breads _____ _____ _____ _____				
Condiments _____ _____ _____ _____				

	Who Pays?	Deposit	Balance Due	Total Expense
Desserts				
Beverages				
Decorations				
Entertainment				
Equipment You Will Need to Provide				
Services You Will Need to Provide				

Total Cost of Rehearsal Dinner $ _____

(Transfer this total to the last worksheet in this chapter)

Use this page to staple any business cards, notes, copies of contracts, brochures, menus, bids, etc.

Rehearsal Dinner Guest List

Name	Address	Telephone Number

Prewedding Snacks

You will need to provide some kind of nourishment for the nervous wedding party, especially for those who arrive early to dress at the church or synogogue.

If it is a morning wedding, you may want to provide a continental breakfast of coffee, juice and rolls. If the wedding is later in the day, any finger foods will be fine. Just be sure they aren't drippy or messy. This is the rule of thumb: "Don't serve anything that will slurp, slip or slop." Small finger sandwiches are good, as well as cookies and fruit. This snack should be light and easy. Make a few things to freeze ahead if you possibly can.

Here is a worksheet to help you plan these snacks. Remember: weddings make everyone hungry except the bride and groom—they won't have an appetite for a couple of days.

Prewedding Snacks

Menu	To be prepared by	Cost
Condiments	**Source**	**Cost**
Beverages	**To be prepared by**	**Cost**

Paper Products Required (paper plates, cups, forks, napkins, etc.)	Source	Cost
Equipment Required (coffeepot, hot plate, etc.)	Source	Cost

Total Prewedding Snack Expense: $ _____
(Transfer this total to the last worksheet of this chapter)

Food for Houseguests

If you ever don't feel like having houseguests, it's when you're having a wedding, but they come anyway, complete with their party spirit, bubbly enthusiasm and hearty appetites. Depending on how many of your relatives come from out of town, of course, you may not have a big crowd "hanging out" in your home, but if you do, the best advice I can give is to go to your friendly wholesale food outlet and buy trays of lasagne, tubs of prepared salads, frozen desserts and breads.

Believe me, if ever you need easy-to-prepare, but delicious, food, it's when you're sitting eight extra people at your table several meals in a row. Or, you can cook up a few batches of your favorite "feed-an-army" recipes! I like to make up Crockpots full of split pea and ham soup, giant kettles of chili or several quarts of spaghetti sauce. Whatever is "your thing," cook it up in advance and freeze it, because right when you're busy with the last-minute wedding details, you need a break!

Use the following worksheet to plan ahead. This way you'll be nice and relaxed when their tummies start to rumble, and they'll think you're some kind of wonder woman to have all that "homemade" food hot and ready for them!

Food For Houseguests

	To be Prepared by	Can Be Frozen Ahead?	Cost
Breakfast Foods			
Luncheon Foods			
Supper Foods			
Snacks			
Desserts			

Total Houseguest Food Expense $ _____

(Transfer this total to last worksheet in this chapter)

Bridesmaids' Luncheon (If Hosted by the Bride)

The last miscellaneous food idea to plan ahead is the bridesmaids' luncheon. This luncheon is traditionally held on the Saturday before the wedding and there is sometimes an exchange of gifts. The bridesmaids may give the bride a gift and the bride will probably give each attendant something personal—usually jewelry that can be worn at the wedding.

It is very common for the cost of this luncheon to be shared "Dutch treat" by all in attendance, although it may be paid entirely by either the bride, the maid of honor or the bridesmaids. This little luncheon can be held in a restaurant or a home. It is the duty of the maid or matron of honor to be sure this luncheon date is set, but it is not uncommon for the bride herself to host it.

If the bride is hosting this luncheon, use the worksheet that follows for estimating the total cost, whether it is being held in the bride's home or not.

Bridesmaids' Luncheon
(If Hosted by the Bride)

Location of Luncheon: _____

Address: _____

_____

Telephone Number: _____

Contact Person: _____

If being held in a restaurant, estimated cost per person: $ _____

Or, if being held in the bride's home, the following estimates:

	Source No. 1	Source No. 2
Menu		
Beverages		
Paper Products Required		

Total Cost of Bridesmaids' Luncheon: $ _____
(Transfer this total to the last worksheet in this chapter)

Final "Other Food" Worksheet

	Who Pays?	Deposit	Balance Due	Total Expense
Rehearsal Dinner				
Prewedding Snacks				
Food for Houseguests				
Bridesmaids' Luncheon (if hosted by bride)				
Other				

Total "Other Food" Expenses: $ _____
*(Transfer this total to **Master Budget** in chapter one)*

Things to Remember

- ❧ Selected a rehearsal dinner food plan?

- ❧ Completed the seating chart?

- ❧ Invitations mailed?

- ❧ Place cards prepared?

- ❧ Financial arrangements made?

- ❧ Planned a menu for the prewedding snacks?

- ❧ Prepared and frozen these snacks ahead?

- ❧ Planned a menu for your houseguests?

- ❧ Prepared or purchased and frozen these foods ahead?

- ❧ Planned the bridesmaids' luncheon (if hosted by the bride)?

- ❧ Purchased gifts to give at this luncheon?

8

The Music

Imagine a wedding ceremony and reception without music! How flat! How boring! It would be about as exciting as a nap.

Music is the glue that holds all the pieces together—the flowers and the flounce, the ribbons and the rice, the dress and the "I do's." The strains of the violin or the strum of the guitar—these are the subtle wooings that bring a tear to the eye and a lump to the throat. You may be counting on an organ that shakes the pillars as the bride walks down the aisle on the arm of her dad; and you must have a reception hall that shouts with the same joy being felt by all.

If you have a healthy budget to spend on your music, you won't mind paying the going rates for musicians. Union vocalists may charge $100 each, a harpist $150 an hour and an organist $110. Your reception music will run the bill up even higher by the time you pay a professional four-piece group $1,500 or hire a disc jockey at $750. These costs can go even higher if you decide to hire a larger or more prestigious group. It isn't uncommon to spend $10,000 on the reception music alone.

Now, for those of you on a tight budget, have no regrets! You can still have quality music of your choice on your small budget by using one of the cost-cutting ideas detailed in *How to Have a Big Wedding on a Small Budget*. One idea, of course, is to use a talented friend or relative who donates one or two musical selections. Another idea is to combine this free talent with one or two paid musicians, such as the church organist. Some brides even use prerecorded music for the ceremony and reception, which is one of the least expensive ideas.

I have provided one worksheet at the end of this chapter. Use it to keep track of all your musicians, whether they are to be paid or not, and the musical selections to be performed. Here are some common musical selections used during the ceremony and reception:

Prelude Selections:

"Arioso" by Bach
"Larghetto" by Handel

"Adagio" by Liszt
"Fugue" by Bach
"Festival March" by A. Foote
"Panis Angelicus" by Franck
"Choral in G Minor" by Bach

Processionals:

"Aria in F Major" by Handel
"March in C" by Purcell
"The Bridal Chorus" from *Lohengrin* by Wagner
"Trumpet Voluntary" by Jeremiah Clarke

Ceremony Love Songs:

"The Greatest of These Is Love" by Bitgood
"O Perfect Love" by Barnby
"I Love Thee" by Grieg
"I Follow Thee Also" by J.S. Bach
"Do You Remember?" by J. Ivanovici
"Morning Has Broken" by Eleanor Farjeon
"What I Did for Love" by Marvin Hamlisch
"Perhaps Love" by John Denver
"We've Only Just Begun" by Paul Williams
"Evergreen" by Streisand and Williams
"The Wedding Song" by Stokey
"You Needed Me" by Goodrum
"Feelings" by Albert

Recessionals:

"Wedding March" from *A Midsummer Night's Dream* by Mendelssohn
"Prince of Denmark's March" by Clarke
"Ode to Joy" by Beethoven
"March" from *Judas Maccabaeus* by Handel

Reception Music:

Here are some of the most popular "first dances" for the bride and groom:
"Just the Way You Are" by Billy Joel
"Endless Love" by Diana Ross and Lionel Ritchie
"Stand By Me" by Ben E. King
"I'll Always Love You" by Taylor Dane

If you decide to make up prerecorded tapes for your reception, you can use the following worksheet to compile a list of your musical selections.

Prerecorded Tape Selections

Activity (Receiving line, buffet service, dancing, cake-cutting, etc.)	Musical Selection	Performed By

Always check with the clergyman or rabbi before planning the ceremony music. There are various rules you may need to follow. Some religious denominations, for example, don't approve of the traditional wedding march. Others will not allow secular music at all. You will also need permission to use the sound system.

If you are stumped for ideas, ask the church organist for suggestions. Church organists have usually played for a variety of weddings and can help you decide upon selections suitable to the formality of your wedding.

One last word of advice: Be careful that you don't use music as a "filler" or as mere entertainment during the ceremony. The ceremony music should be selected for its meaning and solemnity. If you have some clever musical ideas in mind, save them for the reception.

Final Music Worksheet

	Who Pays?	Deposit	Balance Due	Total Expense
Ceremony Musician No. 1 Name _____				
Ceremony Musician No. 2 Name _____				
Ceremony Musician No. 3 Name _____				
Ceremony Musician No. 4 Name _____				
Reception Musician No. 1 Name _____				
Reception Musician No. 2 Name _____				
Reception Musician No. 3 Name _____				
Reception Musician No. 4 Name _____				

	Who Pays?	Deposit	Balance Due	Total Expense
Reception Band Name _____				
Sheet Music				
Equipment Purchase/Rental				
Other				

Total Music Expenses: $ _____

*(Transfer this total to **Master Budget** in chapter one)*

Things to Remember

- Selected your ceremony music?

- Cleared your ceremony music with the clergyman or rabbi?

- Selected your reception music?

- Made financial arrangements with all professional musicians?

- Purchased any necessary sheet music?

- If you decide to use prerecorded audio tapes at the reception, have you completed a list of musical selections?

- Have you arranged to purchase, borrow or rent any necessary sound equipment?

9
Decor

Your ceremony and reception decorations require a creative spirit, a wild imagination and a wide open mind; this is the one place where you may decide to break away from tradition completely. Following a theme, the decorations will establish a certain "feeling" and ambiance. The theme is determined by two things: the degree of formality you would like and the availability of decorative items.

Your first step is to choose a theme. You can use the same theme for your ceremony and reception, or you can use a different theme for each. If you need help in choosing a theme, refer to *How to Have a Big Wedding on a Small Budget* where I explain ceremony and reception themes in detail, including the types of things you will need to purchase, rent or borrow in order to pull it off.

Here are worksheets to help you plan your ceremony and reception themes:

Ceremony Decor

Theme: _____

Items Needed	Source	Telephone Number	Cost

Total Cost of Ceremony Decor: $ _____

(Transfer this total to last worksheet in this chapter)

Reception Decor

Theme: _____

Items Needed	Source	Telephone Number	Cost

Total Cost of Reception Decor: $ _____

(Transfer this total to last worksheet in this chapter)

If you are pulling a theme together on a budget, you will need several volunteers to help you out. Of course, you will need help with the actual decorating itself, usually on the day before the wedding. You will also need help with the transporting of borrowed, purchased or rented items, such as park benches, a portable gazebo, Tiki torches, etc. Use this worksheet to keep track of all your helpers.

Name of Volunteer	Address and Telephone No.	Duty

Use this page to staple any business cards, notes, copies of rental agreements, color swatches, bids, etc.

Final Decor Worksheet

	Who Pays?	Deposit	Balance Due	Total Expense
Ceremony Site				
Reception Site				
Exterior (Driveways, walkways, etc.)				
Interior (Powder rooms, etc.)				
Do-It-Yourself Supplies				
Candles				
Ribbons				
Balloons				
Rental (Gazebo, arches, aisle runner, fountain, etc.)				
Other				

Total Decorative Expenses: $ _____

*(Transfer this total to **Master Budget** in chapter one)*

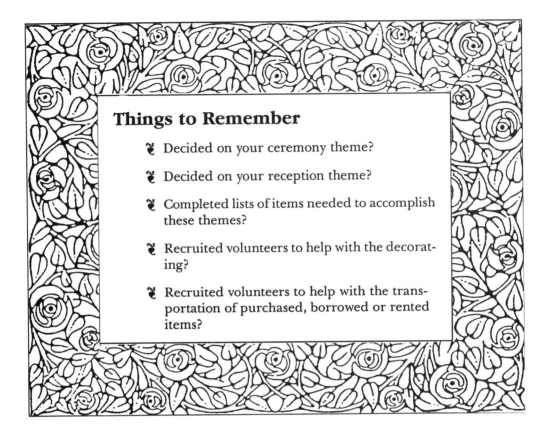

Things to Remember

- ❦ Decided on your ceremony theme?

- ❦ Decided on your reception theme?

- ❦ Completed lists of items needed to accomplish these themes?

- ❦ Recruited volunteers to help with the decorating?

- ❦ Recruited volunteers to help with the transportation of purchased, borrowed or rented items?

10

Photography and Videography

The day after the wedding can be a depressing letdown to the families of the bride and groom. The cake is a memory, the guests have gone home, and the flowers are as tired as the mother of the bride. There is a delightful cure, however, for those post-wedding blues: the moments captured in photos and videotape.

Photography

As you have probably already discovered, professional photography can run well over $4,000 by the time you purchase a complete bride's album and two parents' albums. However, there are ways to cut these costs, detailed in the *Big Wedding on a Small Budget* book, but here are a couple of cost-cutting ideas.

The biggest savings, of course, is to use an amateur photographer. Another idea is to find a photographer who charges by the hour instead of by the "package deal." This type of photographer charges only an hourly rate to photograph the wedding itself, and then hands the film over to the bride's family that day and leaves the rest up to them.

Use these worksheets to compare photographers' bids and your own cost-cutting plans.

Comparison of Photography Plans

	Possibility No. 1	Possibility No. 2	Possibility No. 3
Name and Address of Source			
Name of Contact Person			
Telephone Number			
Number of Hours			
Number of Proofs			
Base Fee			
Formal Portrait Fee			
Album Costs			
Costs for Additional Prints			
Cost of Film, if not furnished by photographer			
Cost of Rental Camera Equipment, if not furnished by photographer			
Cost of Film Processing, if not provided by photographer			
Other Expenses			

	Possibility No. 1	Possibility No. 2	Possibility No. 3
Advantages of This Plan			
Disadvantages of This Plan			
Other Notes and/or Special Considerations			

Final Photography Worksheet

Name of Photographer: _____

(Amateur or Professional) _____

   Address: _____

_____

   Telephone Number: _____

No. of Hours: _____

Arrival Time: _____

No. of Proofs to Be Furnished: _____

Date Proofs Will Be Ready: _____

	Who Pays?	Deposit	Balance Due	Total Expense
Photographer's Fee				
Formal Portraits				

Albums
Bride & Groom's
  No. Photos _____
  Sizes _____
  _____
  _____				

Bride's Parents'
  No. photos _____
  Sizes _____
  _____
  _____				

Groom's Parents'
  No. photos _____
  Sizes _____
  _____
  _____				

Individual Prints
  _____
  _____
  _____				

	Who Pays?	Deposit	Balance Due	Total Expense
Camera Equipment Rental Expense				
Film Expense				
Film Processing Expense				
Other Expenses				

Total Photographic Expenses: $ _____
*(Transfer this total to **Master Budget** in chapter one)*

Videography

Be sure to have your wedding videotaped, not only because it is a safeguard in case the photographs don't turn out, but because every couple deserves the joy of having a video memory of their big day. Videography, or videotaping as it is called, has become so affordable and popular these days that at least one person in every family seems to be into this new hobby. For the tiny price of a good videotape, you can have hours of live recording, complete with voices, music, sounds and antics. Your wedding video will become a family treasure!

If you decide to use a professional videographer, you will pay between $300 and $1,000, with additional costs for special editing or music and graphics added to the master copy.

If you want to hold these costs down, however, you can use one or more amateur videographers who have their own video cameras. Or, you may want to rent a quality camera for someone to use to assure excellent quality. There are also some reasonably priced videographers available, too, but you have to ask around to locate one. You might try your local university for ideas; there are many hungry students out there who make spending money by videotaping weddings, usually for $200 or less. In any case, be sure to use the highest quality videotape you can buy.

Here is a worksheet to use when comparing videography plans.

Comparison of Videography Plans

	Possibility No. 1	Possibility No. 2	Possibility No. 3
Name and Address of Source			
Name of Contact Person			
Telephone Number			
Package Fee			
Number of Hours			
Cost of Videotape, if not furnished by videographer			
Editing Fees, if any			
Cost of Rental Camera Equipment, if not furnished by videographer			
Additional Copies of Videotape			
Other Expenses			
Advantages of This Plan			
Disadvantages of This Plan			
Other Notes and/or Special Considerations			

Final Videography Worksheet

Name of Videographer: _____

(Amateur or Professional) _____

   Address: _____

                     _____

   Telephone Number: _____

No. of Hours: _____

	Who Pays?	Deposit	Balance Due	Total Expense
Tuxedo or Suit				
Videographer's Package Fee				
Video Camera Rental				
Costs of Videotape(s)				
Editing Fee				
Additional Copies of Videotape				

Total Videographic Expenses: $ _____

*(Transfer this total to **Master Budget** in chapter one)*

Use this page to staple any business cards, notes, copies of rental agreements, bids, signed contracts, etc.

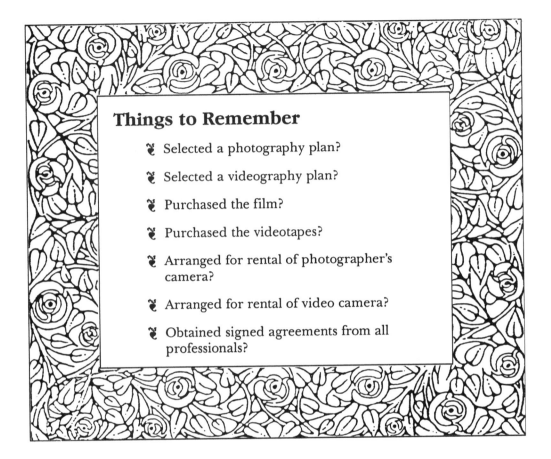

Things to Remember

- ❧ Selected a photography plan?
- ❧ Selected a videography plan?
- ❧ Purchased the film?
- ❧ Purchased the videotapes?
- ❧ Arranged for rental of photographer's camera?
- ❧ Arranged for rental of video camera?
- ❧ Obtained signed agreements from all professionals?

11

Incidentals

Now we come to those aggravating "incidental expenses" that can really add up. Many of these "annoying pests" appear right near the end, when you think you've overcome the worst! My book *How to Have a Big Wedding on a Small Budget* explains how to save money on each of these expenses and how to do without certain incidentals, such as honeymoon luggage, an aisle runner, a makeup artist, a manicurist, a groom's cake, nursery attendants, bride and groom's engraved champagne glasses, a special cake server, limousine service, ceremony programs and a calligrapher. Use the worksheet that follows to keep track of your own unique list of incidental expenses you feel you can't do without. Be sure to enter your total on the *Master Budget* in chapter one.

Incidental Expenses

	Who Pays?	Deposit	Balance Due	Total Expense
Invitations				
Thank-You Notes				
Postage				
Bride's Blood Test				
Marriage License				
Favors				
Last-Minute Alterations				
Guest Book and Pen				
Kneeling Bench or Cushion				
Table Skirts				
Sheet Music for Musicians				
Ring Bearer's Pillow				
Garters for the Bride				
Honeymoon Luggage				
Clergyman's Fee				
Aisle Runner				
Going-Away Outfit				
Makeup Artist				
Hairstylist				

	Who Pays?	Deposit	Balance Due	Total Expense
Manicurist				
Groom's Cake				
Nursery Attendants				
Engraved Champagne Glasses				
Cake Server				
Limousine Service				
Ceremony Programs				
Lighting Technician				
Calligrapher				
Lodging for Guests				
Linen Tablecloths				
Punch Bowls & Other Serving Dishes				
Dry-Cleaning Fees				
Other _____				
Other _____				
Other _____				
Other _____				

Total Incidental Expenses: $ _____

*(Transfer this total to **Master Budget** in chapter one)*

Things to Remember

- Ordered the invitations and thank-you notes?
- Purchased stamps?
- Bride had her blood test?
- Applied for the marriage license?
- Made the favors?
- Arranged for last-minute alterations and pressing?
- Purchased a guest book and pen?
- Rented or borrowed a kneeling bench, if necessary?
- Purchased sheet music, if necessary?
- Purchased or made the ring bearer's pillow?
- Purchased the bride's garters?
- Borrowed or purchased honeymoon luggage?
- Rented or purchased an aisle runner, if required?
- Planned your going-away outfit?
- Arranged for makeup, hairstylist and manicurist?
- Ordered the groom's cake, if necessary?
- Hired nursery attendants?
- Purchased or borrowed champagne glasses and cake server?
- Arranged get-away transportation for the bride and groom?
- Designed and ordered ceremony programs?
- Called the ceremony and reception sites regarding the lighting technician?
- Hired a calligrapher?
- Arranged lodging for out-of-town guests?
- Borrowed or purchased tablecloths, punch bowls, serving dishes, etc.?

12

Your Guest and Gift List

This last chapter will keep you organized in a number of ways. The worksheets that follow for your guest and gift list will do triple-duty because all your information will be in one place. The list will not only keep track of those you have invited, but their RSVP responses, gift given and the date the thank-you card was mailed. By using your guest list to record gifts received and "thank-you's" sent, you will have addresses readily available.

Happy planning and have a wonderful wedding!

Guest and Gift List

Name & Address	Date Invitation Mailed	RSVP Reply	Gift Description	Date Thank-You Mailed

Name & Address	Date Invitation Mailed	RSVP Reply	Gift Description	Date Thank-You Mailed

Name & Address	Date Invitation Mailed	RSVP Reply	Gift Description	Date Thank-You Mailed

Name & Address	Date Invitation Mailed	RSVP Reply	Gift Description	Date Thank-You Mailed

Name & Address	Date Invitation Mailed	RSVP Reply	Gift Description	Date Thank-You Mailed

Name & Address	Date Invitation Mailed	RSVP Reply	Gift Description	Date Thank-You Mailed

Name & Address	Date Invitation Mailed	RSVP Reply	Gift Description	Date Thank-You Mailed

Name & Address	Date Invitation Mailed	RSVP Reply	Gift Description	Date Thank-You Mailed

Name & Address	Date Invitation Mailed	RSVP Reply	Gift Description	Date Thank-You Mailed